Involuntary Vision

after Akira Kurosawa's Dreams

edited by Michael Cross

AVENUE B

Copyright © 2003, Avenue B

ISBN 0-939691-12-4

Editor: Michael Cross

Design: James Meetze
Typesetting: James Meetze & Michael Cross

I am grateful to the poets for their many helpful comments throughout the production of this book

Avenue B
P.O. Box 714
Bolinas, CA 94924

Distributed by:
Small Press Distribution, 1341 Seventh Street, Berkeley, CA 94710
www.spdbooks.org

Contents

Introduction — i

Ryan Bartlett
Rouse — 11

Julia Bloch
Strange Yellow Flowers — 21

Tanya Brolaski
We Disparate Hellenism — 31

Trevor Calvert
a story concerning a discovery — 39

Michael Cross
gamut (for lz) — 49

Eli Drabman
The Dazzle — 61

Geoffrey Dyer
HAND Recent History — 73

James Meetze
How Beautiful, Tragic Weather — 77

Stephen Ratcliffe
from *HUMAN/NATURE* — 87

Cynthia Sailers
The Myth of the Individual — 97

Elizabeth Willis
Dream Anthology — 107

Introduction

Akira Kurosawa's long-running fascination with tragedy is most apparent in his classic films *Seven Samurai*, *Ran*, and *Throne of Blood* (the latter two adapt Shakespeare's *King Lear* and *Macbeth*). Of all Kurosawa's films, though, there is none more artificially tragic, and ultimately didactic, than his 1990 film *Dreams*.

Many would challenge my assertion that *Dreams* is essentially tragic, perhaps due to its *especially* poetic logic (*especially* in the way much of contemporary poetry tends to be particularly Poetic). In *Dreams*, Kurosawa uses sensation (image, sound, ethos, texture) as a throw rug to abscond the film's larger purpose. Often the narrative of the film fractures, and Kurosawa allows the image to trump the plot, as in the many redoubtable "dancing" scenes[1]; however, these scenes are simply devices serving to reinforce Kurosawa's overall objective. In reality, the film is a scathing commentary on the consequences of modern life, our nuclear condition, and our distance from utopian ideals. Kurosawa's film is propaganda, and the problem of his objectivity is at the heart of this collection. In fact, it is the impetus behind it.

The essential problem with tragedy (Kurosawa's and Shakespeare's) is its preoccupation with consequence. Its conclusion is nearly always a snide "I told you so," making of it a perfect didactic tool. In his *Poetics*, Aristotle claims that "Tragedy is an *imitation* not only of a complete action, but the events inspiring fear or pity. Such an effect is best produced when the events come on us by surprise; and the effect is heightened when, at the same time, they follow as *cause and effect*" (italics mine)[2]. Tragedy then is necessarily artificial, and its sole purpose is a sort of learned persuasion. It's a cheap device, meant to lead the reader by the hand, and more often than not, she follows.

The poets in this volume disdain this sort of agitprop affect, even when it's pretty. This is, perhaps, what has earned them the moniker "the New Brutalism" (a term lifted from Ashbery). But as there is no single practice characterizing their work, labels tend to be functionally useless. The writers in this anthology were living and working in the San Francisco Bay Area at the turn of the century (mostly in and around Mills College), and many had ties to such poetry presses as Tougher Disguises, Avenue B, and Manifest Press. The real affinity (labels aside) is that these poets have taken part in an ongoing dialogue with one another, and at the heart of this dialogue is an unwillingness to accept objective conditioning (which, I suppose, gives a label like "the New Brutalism" credence). The poets here are interested in exploring the varied implications of presenting an objective "truth." The question at hand is, what happens when one presents an objective reality, and within the larger scale of presentation, where do we find the most distortion?

We see this line of inquiry in Stephen Ratcliffe's *HUMAN/NATURE* when he writes,

```
                                    woman at microphone
recalling North Tower falling before her eyes, how being
witness is to see it at a distance and also be next to it


man on the right running through cloud of dust, red flames
erupting from behind the triangular slope of Mount Fuji[3]
```

This is a poetry specifically interested in "how" to present an objective reality; it necessarily employs the context or means to examine the effect, and in so doing, unifies context with perception. This is also true in Ryan Bartlett's poetry, in which there is self abasement in the delivery of the line, and a reflexive absurdity in the lyric:

> I would walk in the morning to
> > The middle of their shoot and
> > Ask a question I already knew I knew.
> > I would walk in and watch the marker eat
> > My cupcakes.[4]
>
> And later,
>
> > I am the bonnet on the lady in the background watching.
> > I was once walking and now
> > I am the bonnet on the lady in the background watching,
> > Submissively surprised by my lack of hands.
> > I am a beautiful hand assassin, I always said.[5]

There is a constant sidelong glance at context—at how the speaker and narrative change as a consequence of objectivity. These writers use the "terrible" (the ultimate goal of tragedy) to amplify/subvert its own effects (affects), in order to examine the consequent means. The question is not whether a utopian ideal like Kurosawa's exists, but instead, what is the reality of our contemporary state if we need one?

"New Brutalists" are interested in tragedy the way motorists are interested in five-car pileups. Their poetry is essentially "monstrous." Aristotle writes, "Those who employ spectacular means to create a sense not of the terrible but only the monstrous, are strangers to the purpose of Tragedy; for we must not demand of Tragedy any and every kind of pleasure, but only that which is proper to it."[6] The Brutalists are interested in a sort of hedonism that disregards proportion. There will be no objective moment, no imitative device of *real* life. Neither are they concerned with the sort of didactic propaganda one finds in *Dreams*, especially in "Mount Fuji in Red" or "Village of the Watermills." Instead, the poets here want to make of tragedy a site of investigation—a writing of implications rather than truths. There is no "proper" presentation; there is no attempt at inciting pity from the reader. Instead, they rely on contradiction to maximize connotations. The monstrosity of the work makes the tragedy itself insignificant and smallish.

To a certain extent, these poems are examples of our most popular contemporary art form—the remix; they rework and distill Kurosawa's originals so that certain elements are amplified, while others distort. And while these poets are painfully aware of the terrible in Kurosawa, they choose the monstrous, that irrepressible fact of our social condition. They use the device to call attention to the fact of the device and its horrible out-of-boundedness. There is no objective reality separate from its messy context. The poets here write the context; they maximize both cause and effect, and disallow that tragedy can be explained by trite morals. There is no pity, only an ever-pervasive fear written over and over until it is neutralized by the fact of fear itself.

Michael Cross
Oakland, July 2003

---

[1] See the first two vignettes of *Dreams*, "The Fox Wedding" and "The Peach Orchard."
[2] Aristotle, *Poetics* (Hill and Wing, 1961), p. 70.
[3] See p. 93 of this volume.
[4] See p. 13 of this volume.
[5] See p. 15 of this volume.
[6] Aristotle, *Poetics* (Hill and Wing, 1961), p. 78.

Involuntary Vision

Ryan Bartlett

Rouse

One day,
I would walk in a room
And see a marker and a man,
The same thing essentially
Makes them sigh.
I would walk in the morning to
The middle of their shoot and
Ask a question I already knew I knew.
I would walk in and watch the marker eat
My cupcakes.

Walking in is a matter of habit.

Angela has an idea
That I will be dead
And I will like it more
Than I know that I will.
And she will walk in and still expect
It would have happened on a different day
When the air had a thicker face
When it walked in to give me a life
History I wouldn't want to tell.

There once was a day, man,
When I walked in on you
Giving the Gettysburg
Address to someone
I would want to know.
I was a picture. I was the center.
I am the bonnet on the lady in the background watching.
I was once walking and now
I am the bonnet on the lady in the background watching,
Submissively surprised by my lack of hands.
I am a beautiful hand assassin, I always said.
I am mostly inanimate and I am breathing.

This is a day I wouldn't imagine happening again unless
It happens again.

Mary Todd has always said
I am giving up on the Andes.
I supposed she was just about
Family friends.
I supposed too much and
It didn't give.
I supposed she was a bit depressed about
Her mad sores.
She is still sore and
You are still dead,
The horse doctor said.
I suppose too much to believe
You are dead.

The room has really changed.

Stephanie, as some vague beast,
Is wailing you away.

Her Sheba seems to be misplaced.

And your headshot on the wall
At home is not the same.

She is thinking it
In pieces,
Missing you
In body parts.

Your stillness,
A hieroglyphic,
Is much stranger
Than language.

Amend him
From his risky
Fingers!

Embarrass him
From his infamous
Hemoglobin!

I am the Last of the
Seven Scientists,
Inventing
The unbeatable,
Foreseeing new
Adhesives,
Dissecting
Salt from
The hands
Of applicant
Mammals.

I consume you
Too much
To a T,
My Complete
Impossibility.

You are so
Much so soon,
The Body
Impending.

How Did Matt Die,

Stephanie still says,

What determines distance?

How does a desert just disappear?

Where do I have to ask?

Somewhere Someone in some Santa Fe?

The suggestion arrests our phone breaths.

We need the Big Ring,
The invisible verb,
The Mystery for the keeping.

Somewhere he says to
Someone who is unsaid,

You pricked my mutable skin, painting me
Completely,

I am still a trembling from your last
Inkling.

Julia Bloch

Strange Yellow Flowers

1.

How to weather weather.
A body wrapped in
leaves, dancers made
of fog, as if the forest
were rice paper.
*An angry fox came looking
for you.* She held one
bright eye open and
dressed last year like a
wound. We waited
for weddings, a tired
line of flowers around
her forehead, a repeated
climax in light's wood.

2.

Quick there's a row of
dusty girls to make you
cry. Pink shadow in
corner and army
waits for Doll Day.
Bring some of the dark
back with you when
you go. Waving my stumped
wood by remote control,
dancing one emergency
removed, I didn't want
to die, here, wetly
and acute. I looked for
a crowd of blossoms.

3.

There again I've angered
the atmosphere. But there's
still these hips in long
light. It was a flurry
of news, a digital you,
then *the thing itself*.
Sounds as though we're
coughing up snow. As
opposed to all those
blurry lines, I'm just
apartment-building.
We froze up to our
kneecaps. Then broke
through that winter bitch.

4.

Once you loved all my
last lines. Even the red
here grows dark, we come
bathed in it, or we come
at all. I was wet as
a dog. *I'm so sorry, but*
you died in my arms.
Sometimes dream dresses
in fact: streetlight swings
through the window, curves
off a table, and lands thickly
on regiment. Like how I
tried against the art museum
to eat the menu.

5.

A ripening at the throat
& crying at the dialogic.
There was no shortage
of bones in Van Gogh's
constellation. A body
of injury tells a thousand
words in French. *She was a lyrical
socialist.* I remind you how
speech catapulted her
through the scar on the canvas.
She had visual tinnitis, or else
night blindness. Then she said
yes. Could you believe it then,
how the sun bleached the sky?

6.

I went on a little retreat.
Things got all melty.
My voice went flat.
They color radioactivity
on film to catch the sound.
The clouds chased me down.
I got *gaunt as fuck*
& clipped my forehead.
In the dream I was losing
my hair and saying you don't
understand, I'm losing
my hair. I was troping
toward Bethlehem in the
night's astringent light.

7.

The light is a white noise.
I think this blue skirt
ordinary in its loveliness.
We feed on ourselves.
Yeah it was a difficult
year but fame catapults
you up and she's always
had an enormous soul.
I pried myself off Tenth
Avenue back when more
persimmons were in
season. We lie on top
of the blanket to save time
when theory & practice split.

8.

Birds wave their song
up to titled roofs.
Good, clean water
gives way to a fistful
of bells. Man meets
parade. *Why should night
be as bright as day?* There's
no getting around this
sweep of frivolity.
As a sidebar, I can offer
one trick by explication.
See, once I pawed at the
door as a liquid building.
Intersubjectivity was optical.

Tanya Brolaski

We Disparate Hellenism

I. Foxmeade (Sunshine Through the Rain)

I seemed to see several mists among the mist: foxes walking well-timed—and turn angrily—wedding in miniature. There is objective truth, but this is the real science. Artfully strewing about the rays to ride again. And claimed to have uttered the phrase "let's roll" on a diving plane. But he had the vague amount of muzzle on him. Why should I wake to plant this recurring dream? When you are so far blissful on the wake. When there is so much mythology around foxhood. And I can ill afford to pluck our fingers.

II. Iconostasis (The Peach Orchard)

We speak with apples in our mouths, like animated meats. Nothing is worse than the improbable evil twin, our pigness. With her peach shrine my breath, a spy in the brigade. The menacing peaches paused. And so? I'm swearing in the gilded lily, the pansiest of pansy that cried at the behest of blossoms. Baltic's taken her new lover to a green, a green, a green. And tucked her nicely.

What of all these ribbons you're hanging yourself by, whilst adding a third to our private teatime? Your scarf flutters to the pavement entirely duplicitously, you accidentally address us as "Your Excellency." In short, everything was "singly and in swarms" (the gentlemen) or "singly and in throngs" (the flies). I've had it with your French. It sounds sunny, who knew angels flew so low, etc., but we are not passing with our astute Prince every evening. No-no-no. The mouth's agog but the coach is not ready.

III. Now to my Theme! (The Blizzard)

One among our party, dripping even as death
Does the dastardly
The overall barometer dips

Each mauled and
Given a fire outright
Buggering Kurosawa

Slinking along the Seine
We find actors desirable
Slipping out of our collar to the death

To the guild
To the day I drank tea I demanded death
And a fête to celebrate

I made all the cookies to satisfy
The greater blowhole
The slinkier than thou

Although—my horsedrop—ponder attonce
Having no deep star on my ear
Or holy locket to look upon

A tinsel blanket do I look
Abdominable
I bought the cassingle with my own money

You pause for a snack
Now you witness apparent
Now you're apparent longing

Over-clouded selfharmony
Open it, please, open sesame
Now we guys go

Designation of local
I would say the end is pretty seriously nigh
Deadman ponder apounce

I never stopped respecting your daughter
Every mystery you're attracted to
Sail in sleigh

Snow sailing
When predictions about the future are so popular
We neck like it is summer up in here

IV. Dead Arthur (The Tunnel)

The dog demands toll of its tunnel, and claims pink flesh as a deformity. The dog on the screen and the dog in the room express themselves classically—the blue face & the blue shadow—until swiftly they reach their common climax. Dear dead Arthur, blurred and smeared and candid. You leave money and lights on for ghosts. The newest busboy, vesuvian, smacked to the urgent nature of milky lips. Do they launch to furry fisticuffs? I ate the special cakes, Noguchi, and like the dogs you prove nothing by dying, however mouthing your about-face, you wreck backassed. I willingly concede all supernatural behavior. To the heist of trees, from the ochre acting like "transmittals" happen. What fuss for the bucolic: split pomegranates, feuding f-queens, to whom I dedicate these warsome pages.

V. Redhead Staccato (Crows)

Nothing so much as red wheelbarrows and crows and the red man—no longer an exquisite coxcomb—himself consuming the setting. Redheads have to run from the sun, and luminous pianos abiding—his ear almost as fun a fact as seeing the ancient stars' light. They are deceased much after the cake, the Stendhal Syndrome, the loveletter to Ludwig. Humanity in its treasured threes.

There is nothing "re: this cataclysmic stutter" in my inbox this morning. The best kind of failed art, a coup at the prospect of this lady, as if there were an elegant Lady in the subject of your letter, improvising practiced calm. There is a history in your bed reeking of sundowns. I knew what to do, I chose my one star, and when the clouds were far behind me I spoke not of "galloping" towards the Future. Rather w/ a calm unlike me.

VI. I'm Wild as a Buck Everytime You Calls Me Up (Mount Fuji in Red)

Japan is too small, and inna sick red light. So I glutted (ate) my heart out. It began to leak toward morning, instructing me to Taiwan. Your embrace was almost too vicious. The breaking of certain blood vessels that made the time travel stop. Which I raised in suit to the double engineer, which I daydreamed. No use for fatwas, exquisite weapons, stirring in the embers of Constantinople. What means this fuzzy edge against the grain? The prettiest name, that I ate my heart, and the fact that even Missouri contains a city called "New Madrid."

VII. The Arctic Doldrums (The Weeping Demon)

She swears there exists in the Arctic a paricularly barren and windless region known, straight-faced, as the Arctic Doldrums. So stop your evil curse along the riverbank, the scratching in the background so dead-on. You must think me very innocent. They are running out of night like the urchins light the lamps. "The fault line reveals itself" and makes excellent excuses. We have absolutely no standards, an impeccable memory, stupid gasmasks on the market. To be just stuck, loveless. So I'm pealing with laughter.

Now what does all this catscratch have to do with the doldrums? I've been arcing curves on the quietkey all night. The banjo wrecked me hard. But there's a disco here where the scientists have gathered, there's drinking, there's hands in our warm armpits. I called it "country" but they called it members only. So I'm bleating with my temples, I'm singing to the racehorse, I'm a mudder, one with mud.

VIII. Blind Medievalism (Village of the Watermills)

I am in receipt of your letter, which I am impotent even to imagine. We disparate Hellenism fumbling at the match and the brat country of Priam. I'd fall in streams of liquid only to follow you to sleep, to mimic desire in raw silk. She thought the fervor goes so rapid waiting for the dismount. Whatever that has to do with the pastoral, there being no secrets from the past. What we think of as the past:

O but my heart will break in three
Almost my wit I lose for thee
On water, kneeling one my knee

How should I know if it looks like rain? Unobserved I catwalk the rooftop to the half-bred Ionian, the carver of cherry trees. The blood lab revised of its asbestos. To the windless mills I take no deep drink, though time as always has begun to "creep." Surely your doublet jested when it cast the dice, surely there's a bite to that bark. And the purchase of a gravesite Before Need. Nothing is trivial in space, my man. If you are upside-down there is no right, only blind medievalism. To my free pass you are saying nay, you won't come to the ship but to the drinking with your gossips:

O but my heart will break in three
Almost my wit I lose for thee
On water, kneeling one my knee

Trevor Calvert

a story concerning a discovery

   a gingko leaf splinters light
as mists cover the forest like *oni*
rain sometimes invokes ceremony
and rainbows do not always promise gold
kitsune marry by taking small sidesteps
creating a sense of shallow where deep should be
for each gentle step there is a promise
although a violin's cry will often hide
beneath *kitsunes'* laughter

"What are we to do with this?" the man with all the ribbons cried. His wife, of the pale fingers with square tips, responded, "by looking out the window." "But the wind would like to have a drink by-the-by," all the ribbons declared. Tilting her head, pale fingers with square tips murmured, "Ah. . . then he must take a rain check." She smiled while clouds condensed within her mouth and an umber tail swished beneath her gown.

spring bloomed inside his chest
a pain behind his sternum grew
an orchard unfolding, a flowering
omamori (ringing bit of good luck)
the child hid within his ribs, watching
steps taken that he must
deeply weep and know, must protect
among his family, he alone
knew the secret life of dolls

She of the umber tail swayed in the doorway, waiting for all the ribbons. He was out beyond, and would soon be late for their afternoon tea. "He is probably out meandering again, taking senseless chances with the wind." Soon he had arrived back, said, "Dear, I've brought back peaches from the market." "Peaches are out of season," was pale fingers soft response. Hefting this uncertain fruit, he finally grasped his fortune.

a swirl of white brings comfort
yuki wa atatakai an intrusion of
breath and despair are correlative to
the incline and threat of
remaining, we may breathe—
a profusion of recurring patterns
unaware and mute rhythms
are evoked and the silence
within geometry is absolute

Pale fingers and russet-tail held her balance in the space behind her knees. She sipped her tea, delicately scalding her tongue. Her husband entered from the outside, steaming. "I have misplaced something, covered it with snow. Perhaps I have lost my name." They gazed upon each other's face—watching their breath play between them.

shiryou carries in his throat
askance, a grenade is lodged
stretching lips against jaw
meeting echoes—creating cadence
with precision and guilt
one man's "yuurei banashi"
etched intricate upon
bones and sinews wait for an explosion
feel it only in memory

Small sidesteps echoed as she went searching for her husband. He of the several names had lost himself in that morning's rain, had built a shelter among the reeds. She understood the significance of beginnings and endings, and knew how to find him— would break something and see where the pieces scattered.

a ruptured oracle, an equation sought
cuffed and scattered: his absence mistaken
for loss as clamor of wings intrude upon
fraught observation is what's key, unhindered
the *karasunaki* act in staccato
he cuts his presence, his potential heft
into the diorama reeling
a stroke is made without thought
steps are taken toward noise and sight

Slow sidesteps slipped into her husband's periphery. Controlling her collapse, she sat behind him. The grass shoosh-shooshed. Lost-his-name swiveled, laughing, "Why my dear, you are a most elusive creature!"

an unknowable rift, edit
perfect and hidden
between plunge and sea
fog illuminates the morning
sumimasen said with heavy particulates
explaining clouds and numbers evokes
splendors of hue and desperation
insisting upon mountains and lungs alike
a resolute brevity is called for

They of the hidden gaze and gesture stood at the ocean's border. They culled the air of birds and drove them into the waves. Both understood endings, and took their sorrow when it was necessary.

rubble demonstrated, bifurcated
dust then a looming abscess
kimi wa oni ka? Asked with a sense of
heavy chord and dandelion, grown
swarming and bright, moving against
predation toward a miasma and
he breathing and walking
colliding with his own history
reverberating depth and silence

He was not "full of surprises." He touched her elbow, and she turned toward him. They had grown heavy, saturated with their own noise. "Remember, matter can neither be created nor destroyed," he consoled. They were yet uncertain and both knew they would only grow older. She bit her lip, a bruised daisy, and contemplated the sensations of gravity and impact.

A traveler may stop, observe, but
konnichiwa begins with a flowering
discussion has its every effect
and death may be held by flora and stone
a procession maybe made joyful
cacophony for every query
water is spilled, spun, mended
rhythms made with bells and recollection
a marching funeral singing

They were derived from their context, the circumstance from which they occurred. She had flown, and he who loved small sidesteps pined at her absence. He relied on his "lower senses" and rushed through the high grasses, divining her presence from the breeze. He searched copse, river, and village—all that was left was coincidence. She of the hidden places liked to disappear, if only to be found.

Michael Cross

gamut (for lz)

1

- and could the rain
  made back
  you basilisk
  has square
  our way
  a sudden throat

- some wedding trains
  the rain stop
  at last
  you have a knife so
  the rain stops

- at last you square
  there leaves that stop
  our walking
  at last the rain
  is comforting
  our knees

- of it a lip
  treats the meadow
  to a certain thoughtful
  less you have a knife
  so stop

2

- no leaves in acre felt
  to backspin on the cardboard
  grave of this, my dance poem

- a carbon model
  of the trees
  in my eyelids
  there throbs
  another state
  race ward

- walk my body locks
  thick joints
  wont sleep
  until the city

- their lips no wind
  the eyes
  o decorative orchids
  this is a poem
  about dance

3

- in burdened legs
  and what perhaps made
  heavy
  those projected
  thoughts the snow's
  flat heart

- if there were a spirit
  manifest the mountain aire
  we would naked
  and away in some fashion

- dictated us the booze
  nude because the snow
  is at our knees
  feigns interest in our brutalism
  and we, closeted in air,
  shingling the post
  industrial sector

- "the snow queen's method
  of inducing sleep"
  or "white flight,
  tethered to the legs
  of our contemporaries"

4

- though my echo
  red in the far too
  distorted
  they are not boots
  nor made of rubber
  to be taken in the jaws of zombies
  and basely trounced

- I've come to recognize
  the blue dead
  and decibel
  to be risen in returning home

- said posse cuts a distraction
  apropos hearth
  how am I to apologize
  in such bruiséd face
  amidst the ammunition
  of the live

- the dead w/ assorted backpacks

- concerned with the inability of the dead
  to listen

- *now, as I look at you honestly*
  I would have wanted to die
  however, returning to the world proves nothing

5

- the actor is better train
or yet, the other
side of the camera
a pink in the northwest
canvas of magnets,
the painting river,
colored bricks to point
and laugh our master

- the rays of such plain
made textures
the only life in paints
a sort of spoken
english used
by players and their
brethren wood
made harrow by
the winds thin

- tableaux of earless
assorting, and experience!
art low vulture
heathen thy lapping
of some secret whim
how on the dry docks
you came to know metrics

- and though I am a visitor
in this anecdote
I see and henceforth see
a different light

to reevaluate my
grade school charm
we can make out
seriously
I am abandoned
and only led for crow

6

- they are scared

- suddenly they run fast
  by the hot pink jeep
  and their bikes
  the clouds buzz

- a red one there

- the yellow one
  ten millionth of
  the yellow one
  and his equestrian
  face

- not sure the blow is mine
  nor radio
  active kerchief
  alight the breeze

- and from them fleeing
  so many catastrophes
  in Japanese film

7

- I am to be innocent food
when there cant
like glacier
runs to the things
The Desolation Ruins
a kind of weepy brush
and so lurking
some embarrassed by
the martial life
stupid mankind-like-iceberg
I'm sorry for the nuclear
made night hurts
of a single horn

8

for Great White

- spellcasted in the naming
is a sedentary engine
lit in weed
dying in the village on
the first day by the rock
is a common shrift
from the keyboarded rooves
of the rock and roll

- The Desolation Ruins are coming
on the right day!

- and my parade is near
because I live!
to tell about the things
you sew by leaving
children in the woods
now shrubbery
and slither near the wall
for free

- a clove
the moodiness
of clubbing flames

Eli Drabman

The Dazzle

1.   Spikes come up out of the floor.
They seem to be a commentary on
what used to grow there. It isn't that
I haven't the interest, it's time I lack

and with the now approaching with such
consistent rapidity, I find myself stuck.
Is my own insistence powerful enough
to counteract such a violent clamour?

Are the headaches I've been having
evidence of emerging genius or just
another clue that I've taken the wrong
path? Two paths in a wood tongue

at one single path, and I am on it,
and never will those two paths
or those who walk them forget
from whence they came, nor

the single path ever relinquish
its stream of constant potential,
save if fire or many dry seasons
followed by a monsoon rain

turn the whole forest to dust.
And that is not an option, though
taking things that far can often
save us from forgetting that as much

walking as we do, through the forest
of the city or through the morning
of the wood, anyone can just
take a seat, step aside, or spur

the mechanical horse right on
over the lip of the canyon. And
maybe you'll be on its back,
maybe not, when it goes over.

I just don't think it's a choice
anyone knows they're making
at the time they're making it.
The things I make in time

throw up the razor-sharp
dazzle when harping on
the way I planned for my
feelings to progress. Half

the time, I can't even make
sentences correctly because
it seems never clear how
to stop and make some

thing cut through, that
lasts, without throwing up
a dazzle against the dazzle
ostensibly to pay my vast

respects, but really out of
some sort of spite that I
can't ever be there, don't
know how to stop giving

myself a hero's welcome
every time the poem makes
an embarrassment of itself
beside what might be real.

2. A cat sleeps in the sun
    on top of a bookshelf
    and I am waiting to
    discover it. For the

    sake of everything I've
    waited for and wanted
    in the pasts I've come to
    shun, willing now to climb

    some high place, lie down
    in a warm mess of sunlight
    and wait there til the people
    call me lazier than ever.

    But what people? And why
    must they peek up and out,
    always asking what the hell
    I'm doing with the cat?

3.   I love the way your brown hair looks,
having extended its tips so far
from the hard part of your
head. But for now let's speak

of these things, our mouths and
what they touch, only as much
as we can and will. Only enough
to let ourselves know that there is

still something capable of losing
itself in the gush of discourse
streams and imaginary time.
A place where every

being with language finds it
inescapably pleasant to say
only exactly what is meant
at any given moment.

Utterly avoided, still it waits,
a suit of clothes ready tailored
for one specific person, in one
specific time, to look just that way

in such a perfect suit. You might
need this where you're going,
so take it with you. Friends
have mentioned that there will be a

time when the voices I crave
simply don't go. The poems
then become longer, feel more
confident of getting their way.

4. A day to begin brushes,
    then takes one step back,
    then brushes again like
    some sort of fencing

    exercise. It's not me.
    It can't be. I have no
    interest in breaking in,
    other than simply going

    where I'm tall. I swear
    I'll listen to anyone, just
    point your finger or look
    my way when you're, um,

    talking to hurt my feelings.
    And I'm trying only so hard
    to get these things done as
    quietly as might be possible.

5. The counting experience resumes
as possibilities assume several
different disguises. The blades
fall all around, the spikes.

I'm dancing on them.
In my hands, a big
piece of paper that
catches the food

as it too falls. In this way,
we carry a conversation,
covering each other up
in blank stares & leaving

that other shit right there
for the purists. Cloaked
in the ocean's only black,
really more of a navy

blue, the galleons came
shifting in that day, burned
to a crisp in the storm's
middle and floating now

on their skeletons. Momentarily,
the entire city philosophically
questioned the appropriateness
of the ongoing war. What can it mean

that our voices freeze in air?
That our throats feel as if
warm air touches them
they will break? Memory's

part is really very slim, though
weathering a storm of human
bones is bound to make
man a speaking object.

6.   The people and the places
never roll into one. No,
they don't. And the girls,
for they are separate

from the rest, don't just
stand around swallowing
the flavor from their chewing
gum. If it was only that then

how could any of it crisp
to the point of breaking?
And how could the bashful
boys grow skittish again

only to kick up a cloud
that hides them in a dust
which, someone on TV
always says, ever returns

unto itself. Personally, I'd
rather return to something
less dusty, though it's true
the dazzle of identity with

some one or thing rarely true
plunges arrowheadlike,
cured just with whiskey
and a coal-tipped wing.

7.   I'm unable to make these
kinds of choices, the kinds
that make one resonate with
adulthood, and so I spend

long days justifying
dance on the oblique
edge of adolescence.
Sequined material is cut

from dresses & scattered
all around, along with
the peanut shells from
a dead ballpark back

when its breeze still
burned major-league
fingers. Without asking
for a place to stay in

eternity, nor for some
kind of special glasses
to keep me from seeing
what dangles me over

points of specificity, why
waste time asking for
nothing when so clearly
something is needed

to take up the spaces
left by what we have
removed? A will
comes washing.

8.   Far past the point of fatigue,
       a longing still exists. It is there
       for pleasure's sake, and pleasure
       always lasts for more

       than a moment. What hurts
       recurs, too. The shifting
       or bending back too far
       of limbs. The pulling

       of tooth or strand
       of hair. Different
       strains are braided
       together, different

       qualities of experience
       to make one smooth,
       formally consistent
       pattern of mistakes.

       The guidebook says,
       stop trying to win.
       There's parting fog,
       an ocean, close

       with a density
       of living insides
       kneaded by an almost
       circular moon. The sea

       wants us to use it.
       Wants that we taste
       some salt and see
       one thing, together.

Geoffrey Dyer

HAND Recent History

We have seen this film more than once. That time in my coalescing office, your fading shoes said my old stuff was better, no offense to the fleeting trance. In our beleaguered journey into the woods, eager to casually share the glance of any form, at least conceptually. Fastening such dramatic upholstery to what we couldn't spell, and chasing our teacher's ghost on the roof. It is gray but it is higher. And I have no way of knowing what climate up there. But I bet it's as seen, the indiscriminate rabble suspended in mighty large open. Giant tea. Then came to this, with a beautiful careful of structures. "This novelty has a startling reflex." How all some and such. To place out the letters.

This message carried out through the dark: it's up to you to turn on, latching myself to this wide, solidified in the done. The conviction of a mother is irrevocable regardless of who it is to—the universe been, hackneyed perspiration, an anklet of flow, or mirror men off peddling sedation in search of rainbows. Who wants to say now, are you aware of this orchard I am after?

Divided by the notion of escape, terminal evacuation is the perfect opportunity for closeness. Abolished storm furnace underweighing the induction families. Towards survival, collaborative ones & primitive egg. She can speak so.

The promissory wordless monologue sailors, science's choreography a bitter pilot at best. Mad moments beneath the slits in our face. Decommissioned circle collapse—the refuge concept, we wished to understand it. A more direct line will only eradicate the snow. But the rescuing illusion is unleashed, so try walking away from the chaos.

This is the moment we are invited to acknowledge death, blow through dark circles. In old and the new, she is pinning me to lucid snow.

Echoing dog carrying recent battle, I'm getting tired for trusting off my platoons to you. I can't tell you minstrel, with that much clinging to you. While for the hay, these indeterminate pastures. Requisite egret presence, I'll settle for crows in mine. What happened was I got ahead, you scolded, burying my recent manuscript deep in the yellowed walls. Always returning to what I imagined in your fist, the characters slowly fall to the table. One word for a clouded story. Series of.

Each mine was getting closer to thirst; petals filled the air in obligatory weight and disbursement, randomness figuring in the moving veins of land. Put out there to get knocked over and believed. If only missed sour hardship could have viewed the geographic swell, she'd be blind from dehydration too. Dogs roam the vernacular; the rent is through the roof.

In your arms again, everything has been quiet and VHS awhile, a long motion of scarce off-white. What was that radical disintegration plan we rehearsed? You go out the hole in Sam, I sparkle like a gallon of wine. Comes down to pointing our toes at each other descriptively, squaring off on the top edges of the building. Drawing cold smoke out here, at least leaving the stain conscious. Don't be rid of the pallor to do history the service.

Leaning out the front porch, the sagging view alters the borders of visual sensation. To hold still and see one thing, what does this mean? The plasticy angels in the garage weep malleably. Driven beyond sundials, it tumbles from rotation to be caressed by interference. Let's hope the bankshot through relative skies isn't too alienating.

Here with different rules, observe and change nothing. The harmony oblivious is separate. In different ones you did good things too. But here the water moves without you. And no one notices you, how anachronistic you look, no one says much. Their town, its resources and creations are a rigid interface. Go carve miniatures out of the fragments of space—she's indifferent to cowboy acts these days.

James Meetze

How Beautiful, Tragic Weather

i.

When you are a young boy,
the mist and rain are more curious:

you might follow this desire
to a secret procession.

You come to a tall garden, prefer
a masked fox to self-infliction.

I think of the sharp edge,
considering it is wet and you are a boy

in an endless present, seeking precision,
sure footfalls, painted silk gowns.

I wanted you masked,
grown and animal, we'd think "cunning"

little fox in the meadow, gone to seek
atonement for a blade.

ii.

The dolls are in the trees and the fresh-faced girls—
eager for ceremony or plain experience—

are wrought with some other preoccupation.
I see an island, a blanket of petals and can't

seem to place it, this particular day, these palisades
falling into a snowy glade. There is a thought and

a hypotenuse: I have never run into an orchard
and been scorned, nor approached a girl without dolls

in her closet. I lay down with the southern range,
the trees make the slope beautiful.

To dance between terraces with any
somber creature, what night is different than this?

Where we could fade into ornament, smudge this sky
in star-crossed tongues.

iii.

Build a bigger peak if you want to die climbing it.
So comes sleep in thin-thin time, casting a dress

I'd love to see you in if I were awake. The nearer
you look to the way I inhabit this precise moment,

the more easily its origin in your memory. There is no
snow between us. No vision in the night further than a holiday

for swift addresses. The living tempo that escapes me
within this shunting world. The knock-knock of attraction

I answer perhaps a little too intently. I should not sleep here
in this cold bed, the storm mounting day after day. Death

is swirling over the bravest of strangers in its blue-sky way.
I am seen directly in deviation from route, doing always

the wrong thing. Where instinct, sharp as a mountainside
is never enough to keep me off my back.

iv.

No dancing while the world is ending.
No nuclear family photo melting in the heat.

I saw a small island cry when the lights went up,
sewn to the sky, everything going up at once.

She looks impressive and incredulous, a rocket
without a planet. I am pale in the red clouds rising to meet her.

She's pretty good, she's paramount. Going away from
what explosions knit the possibility of dying, sigh.

The kindness of our atmosphere raining down a carpet
of amnesty. No safety in disaster.

I saw her walk toward a cliff's edge clutching a baby,
then she was gone. Without a grasp of an image

there is only conclusion. There is the boom, the panic,
the quiet desperation in tragic weather.

v.

I had wanted to ask you what a horn
was doing causing you to cry,

when love was a doomed mutation
growing from soot.

Where on this moraine, there is no celebration
for beauty because it is false:

Nobody in my family knows
the new day from the painful season.

A grown boy puts belief to bed and runs
because he is frightened of such anomaly,

roaming to avoid consumption.
I would insert an endearment here

but there is no one I can think of
to call my deep parade.

vi.

You've come a long way to get home
and the dead are breezy. Who came

through your tunnel and asked a favor?
What rotten dogs. Hallelujah.

Every breath a memory in a thing of war.
I don't want to tape myself behind

a warning and be afraid. Everyone's going
home opposite heaven, below a certain intensity of light.

The dream's adrift in a nondescript landscape.
Oh, we're so scared.

Where are the men that do not explode?
That happy-go-lucky feel of walking a path

in prospect of reaching a destination.
Traversing askew in order to grieve.

vii.

You follow because you know the landscape
so well, the bridge, the water wheel.

You are a museum of dreams of women
clutching buckets at the stream.

I think them beautiful, painterly in their frocks,
gathering notes on distance and perception in the sun.

I wanted for this to be a recurring dream, better
to descend than to give way, though I failed in making

it a masterpiece. Dream is all gesture and you figure,
no place for the anticipation of detail but in death and decision.

In a field of crows—you scatter them into the sky—
for what blackness, bleakness they would make in paint.

Language is living in the image you have forgotten,
you isolate it as you reconstruct from memory.

viii.

Silhouettes where our bodies finally go,
across all the bridges and under stone

a procession because someone has died.
I entreat the boy for answers and a

local history. Let me sojourn far
to resume my last year's aching beauty,

midnight's promise that tomorrow won't come
soon enough and I want out of my skin.

Water everywhere in the sounds we make
quick to grieve the spring rain, before it falls.

The boy is a dream version of me then,
a silhouette leaning to the pre-fact

that I am here in sleep, a meander
in the recognizable stream of wantonness.

Stephen Ratcliffe

from *HUMAN/NATURE*

2.28

white-crowned sparrows pecking up seeds from rectangular table in left foreground, pink tobacco plant flower above it, silver of jet passing overhead

                                              Lucian Freud claiming "my naked daughters have nothing to be ashamed of," noting "not using a person is very much like taking a deep breath"

boy in black and white kimono telling sister to "take this," girl in pink running across in front of green plane, woman in orange and white turning to the left in the left corner

line of grey-white clouds to the left of point, wingspan of a pelican gliding across blue-green plane toward it

3.1

pink edge of grey-white cloud slanting across darker grey sky on right, motion of the flat grey plane below it, blue patch opening in window across from it
                                        Hans Blix thinking Iraq's plan to destroy missiles is "real disarmament," White House claiming "total disarmament is total disarmament"
                                                                   man on right moving through blue-whiteness of falling snow, noting "it's waiting for us to die," woman pushing his shoulders back down into snow
                        white line of jet trail slanting across blue-white sky above horizon to the left of the point, triangular wedge of white water on the blue-white plane across from it

3.2

flatness of horizontal grey plane in window on right, blue opening in grey-white sky above it, green cypress branch slanting across blue gate opposite it

                                        woman on right claiming that Jeffers identified with Euripides, <u>Medea</u> represents horror of war that killed millions of people

man on the left looking at lines of men with white faces marching out of a tunnel, who yells at them "you were all killed in action, go back and rest in peace"

                                                            white water moving in across the celedon green plane in left foreground, diagonal blue line slanting across grey-white plane above it

3.3

grey-whiteness of sky behind upturned curve of pine branch in right foreground, song sparrow perched on birdbath below it, sound of jet passing overhead

                         Lucian Freud claiming he paints people "not in spite of what they are like, but how they happen to be"

                         man with blank canvas in right hand walking into a Van Gogh painting, man on right walking across field toward edge of blue sky, sound of crows flapping up from left foreground

                                 celedon green wave approaching in right corner, rainbow in curve of white spray blowing back from wave breaking to the left of it

3.4

pink edge of cloud above ridge in the window opposite unmade yellow and blue bed, sound of birds chirping in foreground below it, waves breaking in channel

                                          woman at microphone recalling North Tower falling before her eyes, how being witness is to see it at a distance and also be next to it

man on the right running through cloud of dust, red flames erupting from behind the triangular slope of Mount Fuji, man on left claiming cloud of Plutonium-239 causes cancer

                                                        grey-white plane of sky tilting down behind green pine on point, wingspan of pelican flapping across grey plane toward it

3.5

shape of low white cloud moving to the left across blue sky in upper left corner, sunlit green cypress branch slanting across foreground below it, sound of jet passing overhead

Stalin claiming "where there are people there is trouble, where there are no people there is no trouble"
                man running across burned-out slope, smoke drifting up from lower right corner, man on the left recalling "long ago this place was a beautiful field of flowers"
              white line of jet's trail slanting across cloudless blue sky in upper right corner, reflection of sunlight on the blue-green plane below it

3.6

blinding silver circle of sun behind upturned curve of pine
branch in foreground, sparrow pecking up seeds from table
below it, sound of jet passing across blue sky overhead

man on radio noting Prokofiev died a few hours before
Stalin, not a single flower left in Moscow for the composer

man standing beside stream seeing "children putting flowers
on a stone," asking older man in a blue shirt "what about
lights," who asks "why should night be as bright as day"

shaft of sunlight slanting to the left from grey-white
cloud, triangular plane of still dark ridge behind it

Cynthia Sailers

The Myth of the Individual

It is Russian doll day.
Imagine a hypothetical child
Could play with others. Where birds
Guard this city under throes of romanticism.
To describe these circumstances even roughly.

The blood hounds are acting normal
And (off the record) being perverse
Being homosexually English
With metaphysical names
For these new surroundings, engulfed
In free range meat.

The Roman Empire and idyllic love
Are soon displaced by weak adequacy.
Antiquity as you have a nation.

Whatever gooey messages come out
Whatever odd that flows from the abyss
Of the body itself. Or being out
To these sexual organs and their opposites.
You must choose a statue: going to bed
With you upon a wave of nature.

*

Thinking of the larger picture
And flowers on the drunken lake. All the same,
Hunted by their own caricature. The nature
Of tissue on one hand
And a template on the other.

You think there is blue
And its thumbnail print.

As birds fly with tunnel-vision
Coming in and out of insatiable robes.
Eating the primitive compost. All of us
With a juice box.

Sooner or later you don't see the fine points
But our separation from the dream-like qualities
Of snow. The rupture of beauty into
Small shells of intelligence.

Statues and a sea of others some may think
To be real, those who had been living through
Radiant maps. Repetition of nudes
And their illusions.

*

Looking into an iris and these rivers
Of film

Like a colony of imaginary friends. We enjoy
These new lodgings. Symbols
For our private lungs, our illuminated rooms.

Such little birds staring down
Into the simple grass of summer.
Who experience the artificial world,
This paradise.

Next to abstract nation and Japan. A kind
Of numbered life. Clothed by a network
Of right-brain activities: swimming
In a television of mere power, then working
The floor for an electric axis
Of light and submission.

It will soon snow, it is snowing.

*

We never took advantage of the sea,
A drop of squid ink from a crime.

I wanted the explanatory plant. The imperial
Bird descending a slope mediated by
A sign for road work, a sign to require
This station to provide air and water.

To desire the language instinct. An obvious cow
In pastures of warm order. The Army inoculates us,
Our adopted child looks out the window.
I had been driving down to City Hall.

There is base morality and there is the weather.
You have to look hard to see the crows
Shaped into small pieces of paper, turning
Windmills. The classic statues are more baroque,
And time more exaggerated.

I was a huge fan of artifacts when we first
Started dating.

*

There is a rose but not the same as before.
Let us build a sanctuary out of nature.
Whereby huntsmen find the lake
A code of signals. We cannot define
What has brought us, what has been
The dark water covering its surface.

We were once attempting to act like a human
Immune system. I was hording some deer fossils,
Some inner turmoil to be borne again
In the dormitory of light.

There is not enough time to think about astronomy.
Or lessons. There are still too many American
Bird lovers. It is as if they all look alike.

*

I feel like we've lost the effort. Without any overlaying
Structure made of birds or plastic resistance
Of alternating voices. A choreographer who
Harnesses the loneliness. A reason
To say the weather is strong enough
To unroll the ground.

This part of mythology has its symbols. A record
To shut out some of society.
I was alone but still in the city
I watched the lights change position.
Walking down the wrong path
Into a flight of circumference
There is no fountain here only a chair.

Photographs of my double with her real name
Breathing in the grass; this above the turnpike.
There is a grave for the other person.

There is also an enamored pillow in my mouth.

*

The countries of invention. The world is said to be
A farewell. Each time a conclusion is made
A movement to the other side of the room.
How must the inexpressible language be a lady.
With her leftist remarks and hotels that fell
From her hands.

How do we remember all the capitals
While we are idle. This terrace bed
Is mainstream, sex on the level of argument
Where all the elements bloom and so
Luck would have it: a butterfly, a glass container
One in each hand. You resist actually thinking
About social performance, about lack of space
And all the narrative subways.

Can it be that the ducks are barking.
The lake has a face. We are regulating
Its movements identical to the sea.

*

No idiot-boys, no epistemology. Rain again.
On the hill waiting for her email with yellow
Budding flowers. Riding horses in a diorama.
It's all an illusion.

To steer you away from home into private property.
The places you preferred the most urban tiles
And looking back there are ghosts
And a special cake they made there.

But I don't believe in the dead. Standing at attention
In order to be called a hero. Our last chance
To find history. Erased on the level of detail

To the bottom of the sea. Men are working
At the quarry babies crying from chickenpox.
Gathering the symptoms like a storm
On the continent.

There is no way out of Japan. This is the future.
We are the outcome of its fallout.

Elizabeth Willis

Dream Anthology

1.
The tree has an eye
for temporary stardust
It's Tuesday on Wednesday
The woman left you
to wooden shoes
Forget what you see
that never was
Your sweetest georgic

2.
Tingling
little white
girlshoes
He's this
looking machine

3.
The poet is a snowman
his fatal love
It'll soon be night
The ice-bashed hand
in crowded nothing

4.
My metal name looks out its hole
in little steps, of crows
That bleary light
I used to know
the bluest doll
buttoned into clay
Keep this for me

5.
That's the queasy sycamore
that keeps the town
from drowning   That man's
a train, a hungry
bandaged bull against
the grain

6.
Some official end debris
looking for a data body
Her face stars all its previous heat
unmanaging to touch
the tie, the sea
the backward wheel

7.
Wanting to mean
with all his horn
the puns of war
in dandelion shadow

8.
The random village declares itself
an independent blossom
Utopia cannot be seen
but costs you twice
Behind the dream behind the snow
someone closed the greenest door
on artificial islands

Author Bios

Ryan Bartlett is the author of the chapbook *Recovery*. He now lives in New York City with his wife.

Julia Bloch was awarded the Joseph Henry Jackson Award for poetry in 2003 and was a finalist for the Modern Poetry Association's Ruth Lilly Fellowship in 2001. Her first chapbook of sonnets, *Problem-Solving Outline*, was released by Bigfan Press in 2003. She lives in San Francisco, where she works as an editor and writes epistolary poems to Kelly Clarkson, the towheaded winner of last year's *American Idol* reality TV series.

Tanya Brolaski is a PhD student of Medieval and Renaissance literature at UC Berkeley. She lives in Alameda and writes the blog Swimming for Dummies (http://tanyabrolaski.blogspot.com).

Trevor Calvert lives and works in Oakland, where he edits & publishes at Manifest Press. When not reading poetry, he makes every attempt to balance his textual-intake with science fiction and gothic literature (lately, Stanislaw Lem and Charles Maturin).

Michael Cross is a PhD candidate in the Poetics Program at SUNY Buffalo. He is an editor at Manifest Press, *syllogism* magazine, and the monthly public poetry project, Secret Swan. He is the founder of The New Brutalism reading series in Oakland, and acted as curator for the 2002-2003 season. His chapbook, *in felt treeling*, was published by Soft Press.

Eli Drabman was born in Santa Cruz, CA. He received his B.A. from UC Santa Cruz and his MFA in poetry from Mills College. Eli sings and plays bass for the band The Black Plastics. He lives in Oakland, CA.

Geoffrey Dyer's first book, *The Dirty Halo of Everything*, was published by Krupskaya in 2003. He sings and plays guitar in the band The New Faster Bigger. He teaches creative writing to high school students and lives in Oakland.

James Meetze is the publisher of Tougher Disguises Press and co-editor, with Dan Fisher, of the journal *A Very Small Tiger*. He is a letterpress printer and freelance book designer. His chapbook, *Serenades*, is forthcoming from Cy Press. He lives in Oakland and writes the blog The Brutal Kittens (http://tougherthanblog.blogspot.com).

Stephen Ratcliffe's most recent books are *Portraits & Repetition* (The Post-Apollo Press) and *SOUND/(system)* (Green Integer). *Listening to Reading*, a collection of essays on contemporary poetry and poetics, was published by SUNY Press in 2000.

Cynthia Sailers was born in San Diego, CA in 1974. Her first book of poetry, *Lake Systems,* is forthcoming in 2003 from Tougher Disguises Press. Her work has also appeared in various journals, including *Aufgabe*, *14 Hills*, *LitVert.com*, and *pompom*. She received her MFA in poetry from Mills College in 2003.

Elizabeth Willis is the author of three books of poetry. *The Human Abstract* (Penguin, 1995) was selected for the National Poetry Series, and *Turneresque* is just out from Burning Deck. *Second Law*, a book-length poem, was published by Avenue B in 1993.

Involuntary Vision was typeset in 11 point Granjon, with the exception of Stephen Ratcliffe's from *HUMAN/NATURE,* which was set in 9 point Courier. Printed and bound by McNaughton & Gunn in Saline, Michigan.

Avenue B Books

OUTSIDE, Todd Baron, $9.95

Talking in Tranquility: Interviews with Ted Berrigan, Ted Berrigan (published with O Books), $10.50

Japan, Maxine Chernoff, $6.00

REGISTERS / (PEOPLE IN ALL), Clark Coolidge, $9.95

Post Hoc, Michael Davidson, $8.00

News on Skis, Peter Ganick, $8.00

Linen Minus, Susan Gevirtz, $8.00

Words nd Ends from Ez, Jackson Mac Low, $7.50

Amblyopia, Jena Osman, $8.00

Among the Blacks, Ron Padgett & Raymond Roussel, $7.50

Distance, Stephen Ratcliffe, $6.00

Second Law, Elizabeth Willis, $8.95